Cover Design

You can judge this book by its cover. What you see in the list of names on the front and back are sources of influence on me as a leader. Each name is someone who directly touched me in person to shape me. It also includes people I never met personally but whose work, I routinely quote. The list includes family and friends, authors, athletes and artists, famous folks and neighborhood characters. It also includes some people I would consider allies as well as adversaries, some who pushed me to excel and some who blocked my efforts to grow. There is a story related to each one and there are others whose names I do not remember or maybe never knew.

Perhaps there is merit in not locking in on your judgment just based on what you see. Do however recognize that even the outside of a book or the outside of a person is a representation of what lies inside and beneath. Take this cover as an invitation to turn the page and go a little deeper. You will be fine and the cover will have served its purpose. Hopefully you have already begun to think about whose names belong on the cover of *your leadership signature* book.

Greg Pennington, Ph.D.

GREG PENNINGTON, PH.D.

YOUR LEADERSHIP *Signature*

Mapping your personal pursuit of influence and impact

This book is designed to provide accurate and authoritative information
with regard to the subject matter covered. This information is given
with the understanding that the details of your situation are unique.
Engaging the professional services of an executive coach or leadership
development consultant will increase the effectiveness of how you apply
this information to your situation.

ISBN 9798640756081
Printed in USA by Kindle Direct Publishing

Greg Pennington, Ph.D.
404-201-2974 (Office)
drgpenn@pennpointconsultinggroup.com

*Dedicated to my wife Kristy and our children Kalin and Kyle.
I have worked to put my signature on everything I touch and make a difference to everyone I meet.
I am blessed to have you as signs, sources and inspirations of my signature.*

Chapters

In the beginning

I did not think of myself as a leader while growing up. I can recall more reasons not to jump out front than I can encouragement to take the lead. I did not have the research framework and vocabulary then to form a hypothesis of whether I was born to lead, could grow to lead or was destined to follow. My mother reminded her five sons to not think we were better than anyone else and she encouraged us to be our best. There was a hint in her message about leadership, telling us to fit in and not to stand out. I recall trying to explain why I might have gone along with what someone else said to do. To which she said, if someone told you to jump off a cliff, would you? I was wise beyond my years to avoid saying out loud: "it depends…"

I remember one day in the courtyard of the public housing projects where I spent my first 8 years when I took the initiative to jump out front that did not go as planned. To provide more context, I looked up to my older brothers and tried to hang with them and not be left behind like a typical younger brother. On this day, the gang was huddled together because "Bobby Boom Boom Bully" had once again claimed all the swings in the courtyard. My brother was inciting our gang to do something this time and use the strength of numbers and the element of surprise to jump Bobby Boom Boom Bully from behind and…I don't remember the rest of the plan because I took the initiative, being one of the youngest and smallest of the group to get a head start. Off I sped, focused on the mission of jumping our neighborhood, older, stronger bully from behind. Knowing that at any moment the faster and older members of our gang would soon over take the initiative I displayed to get a head start, I leapt a few feet from Bobby B3's back, looked over my shoulder and saw the rest of our group still in the huddle looking at me like I had lost my mind! I landed on Bobby's back and he took the initiative to convert my landing point to my head on the ground! Early leadership lessons learned: Wait for the full plan? A jump start is not always wise? There is strength in numbers? ……

There are THOUSANDS of leadership books published each year. There are millions of leadership stories unfolding and billions of people touched by persons of influence and impact. Mine is just one of those stories. If it did not literally start with Bobby Boom Boom, he certainly represents an early and vivid memory that has shaped my leadership signature! What's your story? What's *your leadership signature?*

Why this and how to use it

A professional colleague who is an accomplished author suggested that if you were to write a book, be clear and realistic about why and what you expect. With the millions of publications available, the variety of ways to claim the moniker of "best-selling author", and the realistic limit to how many copies of my book my family and friends would first purchase, and then second actually read, I want to begin by sharing with you "why" this book, and how I imagined you would use it.

I have had the privilege of being a resource to others in their efforts to understand what they feel, think and do. I have been honored and humbled that I have listened well enough, counseled, consulted, advised, vented, and shared on occasion something that contributed to others gaining enough insight, incentive, and direction to actually do something different. In some instances, doing something different, equated to being more conscious and intentional about choices and consequences. It is that intentionality of effort that increases the probability that you will be able to repeat the behaviors you want to increase, and address the behaviors you want to decrease, eliminate, or replace. I have done this one-on-one, one-on-some, and one-on-many.

This is my effort to capture some of those experiences, insights, and suggestions, and offer them to you in a way that you can access at your convenience. This is autobiographical and unavoidably flavored with my biases and mix of positive self-attributions, samples of growth and effectiveness, and a few slightly sanitized glimpses of where I have struggled, remain defensive, short-sided and/or limited by blind-spots. I considered calling it a book, workbook, journal, guide, or professional development plan. It turned is all of those.

It is also representative of a challenge issued by former American Psychological Association President George Miller to "give psychology away". He pushed psychologists to assure that our research had practical applications, and that it was accessible to as many people as possible. Though most of my professional career has been built around executive coaching and leadership development programs, I am convinced there is significant work each of us can do on our own --- with some guidance. In essence what you have in front of you is me, sharing experiences as a leadership coach including questions and exercises I have used with clients. You also have several glimpses of me as a leader still on my journey defining and refining my own leadership signature.

When I have produced a similar product or been asked to describe an overall process for leadership development, I have referred to the output as an 'accelerator' or 'elevator'. In some instances, I called it an "edge". In my role as a leadership development consultant, I focus my mission on "accelerating and elevating leadership effectiveness". Whether the target is an organization's population of leaders, a team, or an individual leader, the intention has been to identify and drive behaviors that provide an "edge", an advantage, a differentiator between the best and the rest. In one context the organization is striving to select and develop what it might consider high potentials, those most likely to reach the upper levels of the organization and or expanded roles and responsibilities. The organization may also choose to focus on high performers, those who can produce more. In a more individual context, the 'edge' is focused on how can we get each individual to recognize and leverage when they were at their best compared to when they were at their average.

I invite you to use this and me as a reference point regarding the development of your leadership effectiveness. I am not and this is not a benchmark or a prescription. If you passively absorb what is here, actively test how it applies in situations relevant to you, and intentionally adjust and adapt it so it fits you, it will come close to being worth the time and dollars you have invested. It is not really a book to read through as much as one to think through and work through. My colleague Carol said she hates to write in these types of workbooks, preferring to keep her pages clean. If you are like her, I encourage you to pick up two books, one for your library that you can keep clean and one for your work desk that should look and be used.

There is a logic to what's included and where the content is placed. The implication is there is a logical, perhaps even linear flow to developing leadership effectiveness. Trust me, it reads more linear and predictable than it was experienced! I encourage you to read it from page 1 through the end. It may be just as beneficial to dive right into a particular section for whatever reason makes sense to you.

The book maps a journey to defining *your leadership signature*. Each part of the journey, each chapter, offers personal applications to illustrate key dimensions of leadership. It provides exercises, or maps you can use to frame your reflections and insights. The journey begins by outlining how you have already defined **LEADERSHIP**, what you have come to expect from experiencing leadership effectiveness of others. The next chapter pushes you to consider your **MISSION**, making the point that "why" matters. What follows are three critical components of leadership: **VISION**, how you collect, connect, and communicate "dots" or data points; **IMPACT**, what buttons you push driving for results; and **CAPABILITY**, how you get more from more. The next chapter underscores the role of **LEGACY**, what difference you have made to whom in capturing the scale and sustainability of your leadership effectiveness. **SIGNATURE SOURCES**, what and who influenced you as a leader encourages you to list the books and other reading sources that have influenced you as a person and a leader. It also invites you to consider what persons you have encountered that have had notable influence on shaping your approach to leadership. The book concludes with a collection of **PATHWAYS**, the exercises and maps presented along the way. They are a collection of questions I have used in individual executive coaching engagements and in group leadership development programs. Ideally you will be completing the exercises as you work through the book. Copies of the exercises are provided in the

PATHWAYS section to make it easier to find so you can do them again or copy and share with others.

However, you choose to page through it, I want you to appreciate the interplay between a big picture statement or principle and the personal way it played out for me. Suggested actions and activities are included that you might engage in to intentionally drive your understanding, accelerate your development, and elevate and expand your capability and capacity. In a few instances I have included examples of how I worked through the exercises.

Let me share three important disclosures. First, I place a premium on being personal, with an appropriate respect for personal and professional boundaries. A clinical psychology supervisor insisted that I needed to work on my counter-transference, over-identifying with others and projecting my emotions and thoughts onto others. Secondly, in a recent process of certification for an executive coaching program, I was told I needed to direct more effort to asking questions and focusing on the client because I was "too prone to offer personal stories and advice". I am guilty on both sets of feedback, BUT, it works for me. What I really want you to do is find a way to put your signature on your leadership. If I can have some degree of impact on how you feel, think and react to that, I will be satisfying my personal and professional mission.

The third disclosure is that in the body of the book I have changed names of people with whom I have worked, and minimally described any companies I have referred to along the way. They are real people and real companies, and the perceptions and insights I have shared are real as well.

To be who you are and to become all you are meant to be is the only goal worth living.

—Alvin Ailey

Chapter 1

LEADERSHIP

What I have come to expect

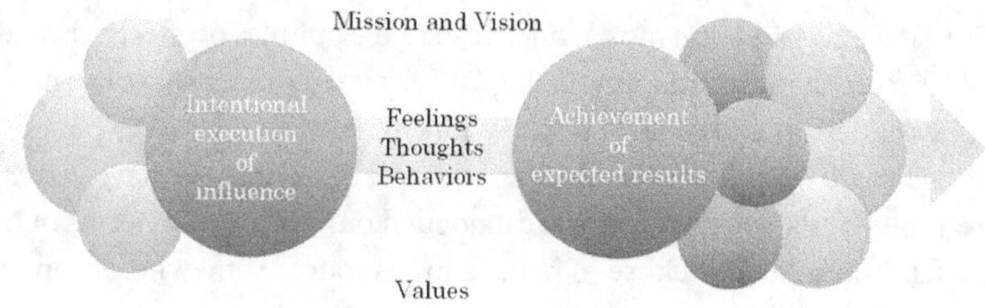

Leaders make a difference

We should begin by defining effective leadership. We often jump into leadership development efforts without defining what we mean by leadership or agreeing with that definition. The illustration of intentional leadership on each Chapter page offers a starting point that attempts to capture some common elements in most definitions of leadership. It begins with the assertion that "leadership is an execution of power or influence". We have choices of how to intentionally execute power or influence. Certainly, the range of choices varies with each person and in each situation. It is also certain that each of us develops tendencies regarding those choices. The intention of those choices as leaders is to impact the way others feel, and think and the behaviors they demonstrate. The objective of those intentional efforts is the achievement of specific observable results.

What is central to mapping *your leadership signature* is defining what leadership means to you. Set aside for the moment how you would define leadership and the model illustrated above. You have no doubt already been exposed to a long list of models. The key point of this journey is to identify those ingredients that resonate with you for whatever reason. Focus first on what are examples of effective leadership for you.

Think of someone who is an example of an effective leader. What did that person do to make you consider them an effective leader?

Even if we consider the most evidence-based examples of effective leaders, we process that information through a very personal lens. We learn from our experiences and model our behaviors in reaction to those experiences. Long before we acquire the language to label behaviors, we have gathered examples of those behaviors and catalogued our reactions in terms of how we felt, thought, and chose to behave in response. Somewhere along the way we began our personal journey to shape how we might intentionally seek to influence the way others feel, think, and behave.

So, who came to mind for you as an example of an effective leader?

Ideally you thought of three to five people immediately. Ideally, they were people who touched you directly. This is not to minimize the power and importance of people you have heard about, read about, wished for or worshipped. They will have degrees of influence on what you expect of leaders and of yourself as a leader. Push for real life, vivid, personal examples because they present a clearer, more credible, and more realistic example of what YOU might expect and are more likely to do.

Why three to five examples? It is important to have enough credible and rich data to uncover patterns. It also provides some insights into the range, diversity and adaptability of implicit models for leadership effectiveness—what common themes are revealed, what subtle yet significant differences are apparent? How do your personal examples of effective leaders influence your definition of effective leaders?

Think of someone who is an example of an effective leader. What did that person do to make you consider them an effective leader? Follow **PATHWAY 1** that to capture your examples of effective leaders. Look ahead to **PATHWAY 1a** to see how I completed this exercise as an example.

PATHWAY 1: EXAMPLES OF EFFECTIVE LEADERS

List the names of 3-5 people you consider to be effective leaders.

Describe the types of roles they filled.

Identify specific things they did to make you consider them effective leaders.

Describe how you reacted to what they did. Consider what you felt, thought, and did.

Consider yourself fortunate to be able to identify multiple examples of an effective leader. It is not uncommon for people to laugh when presented with this question and exclaim how much easier it would be to come up with examples of bad bosses! In addition to preferring positive examples of behavior as a motivator for development, what makes us so sure a person was a poor or ineffective leader is that we have a clear picture and preference for what is an effective example. I would rather choose a journey to be an effective leader than choose one to avoid being a poor leader.

PATHWAY 1A: EXAMPLES OF EFFECTIVE LEADERS – SAMPLE

List the names of 3-5 people you consider to be effective leaders.

- *Larry*
- *Roberto*
- *Sam*
- *Mary*
- *Melvin*

Describe the types of roles they filled.

- *Community activist, a philosopher with a bare-knuckles style*
- *Education leader, charismatic, second generation Cuban American, driven by mission and relationships*
- *Fortune 500 senior leader, humble, thoughtful, decisive*
- *Director of educational program, community activist*
- *Lawyer, first Black mayor, youngest, public officer, family lineage, bold*

Identify specific things they did to make you consider them effective leaders.

- *Exposed people to thoughts and thinkers we did not know; pushed people to connect what they did to a bigger picture; challenged the status quo*
- *High energy, shifted communication style depending on audience, always led with and defended the mission (e.g. students)*
- *Analytical, intentional in being personal, listened, blended independent thinking with interdependent; Gathered information, balanced logic with humble compassionate, leveraged key resources, and retained personal responsibility, willing to compromise, strategic*
- *Passionate, mission driven, relationship builder and connector who leverages them to get things done*
- *Pushed the status quo; Embraced the permission and burden of privilege; connected adversaries and allies, visionary, "a maker", accepting his "privilege" and the responsibilities that accompanied it, knew he could*

step into the fire and deal with whatever might come from it including the benefits and getting burned along the way

Describe how you reacted to what they did. Consider what you felt, thought, and did.

- *Felt inspired and permitted to learn and think; felt protected if we dared to stand our ground; took responsibility to be more direct*
- *Felt connected to him; made me want to have similar charisma and to trust a sense of humor*
- *Appreciated how much trust you have to have in others to bring you good information and how to inspect what they bring; assure that trust is merited, realize that strategic decisions and driving for results could be driven by values; felt trusted and a thought partner*
- *Inspired, personally connected, empowered to do more than expected*
- *Special, connected, humbled, challenged to make the most of what was given, even with privilege, able to make a difference in people and broader community*

Once you have completed your list set it aside for a few minutes and not more than an hour. This will allow you to get a little bit of distance from your thoughts so that your analysis of themes is slightly more objective. It would be even more revealing if you asked someone else to look at the list and identify themes. As an example, you may see patterns and themes in my example that are not apparent to me. You are likely to form early reactions even as you look at the leaders you chose from the longer list of leaders you have had over the years. Some clues are actually in the words I chose or you chose to describe those leaders. What do the people you chose have in common? Are there clusters of behaviors that appear when you read all of the descriptions and the behaviors you identified as what made them effective? What patterns are apparent in the reactions you had to your list of leaders?

Follow **PATHWAY 2** to begin analyzing your examples of effective leaders. Consider inviting someone else to answer the same questions about your examples to provide you with the value of another perspective.

PATHWAY 2: ANALYSIS OF EFFECTIVE LEADERS

What is common in the leaders I chose?

____

____

____

____

____

____

____

What stands out in the way I describe them?

____

____

____

____

____

____

____

Cluster the behaviors you described into specific groups.

Categorize your reactions.

What does the evidence say about effective leadership? What does it say about my personal touch or your personal touch? While I have a reasonable respect for evidence-based theories and demonstrated results, I know that I start with some degree of bias, preference, and frame of reference. You have to convince me with a preponderance of evidence, and equal dose of persuasion for me to come close to a balanced view on some things. I can be hard-headed and set in my ways. There is a part of me that has to exert extra effort and emotional sweat to choose to change my behaviors, feelings or assumptions. So, I confess that I am not easily swayed by researched based models of leadership whether quantitative or qualitative, when it comes to applying those models to how I perceive myself as a leader. I am a student of those models, but more a student of myself. Norms help me calibrate my perceptions and self-assessments. When I have shared assessment feedback with others, their first question is usually "what does that say about me?".

There is an important part of me that would rather use Larry, Roberto, Mary and Melvin or Sam as reference points than simply target a percentile ranking of behavior as my personal target for being as effective as possible as a leader. If you are driven by numbers and rigorous research, take advantage of that as one variable in your efforts to define what effective leadership looks like. Also factor into your recipe those emotional examples you have already incorporated from your personal experience.

Back to your examples or mine. Some themes were being revealed in the process of sorting through all the possible names to consider. Not all of the leaders you have experienced will make your list of 3-5. As you described them and recalled what they did, the outcomes that represented effectiveness to you, and the impact of what they said and did on how you felt, what you thought and what you did, it should become more and more apparent how those memories shaped your journey as a leader. Follow **PATHWAY 3** to capture and use the insights you have to complete the statement: For me, an effective leader is …

PATHWAY 3: INSIGHTS REGARDING EFFECTIVE LEADERS

How would you describe an effective leader?

When I asked earlier for you to think of someone who is an example of an effective leader, did you think of yourself as an example? Would you raise your hand among a group of peers to say so? If so, what do you do that makes you think you are an effective leader?

Also notice that I shifted from defining leadership as an exercise of power to describing it as an exercise of influence. I was asked by a client, if I were to narrow down the essence of effective leadership what one word would I use. Without hesitation my answer was: power! The hesitation and the default to the euphemism of "influence" is part of my personal signature on leadership. As a middle child, with reminders from mom to not think I was better than anyone else, I was reluctant to own or at least label one of my motives as "power". Over the years, I came to appreciate that power could be used for personal gain and for social gains. I also recognize that the notion of power cannot be accurately defined unless it is taken into context. Context includes the family culture in which we were raised, the socio-political climates in which we exist, and the organization culture in which we work. The same caveats should also be considered when you revisit your thoughts about who represents an example of an effective leader.

If you did not think of yourself as one, or would not confess to it in public, why not? Add your thoughts to **PATHWAY 4.**

PATHWAY 4: YOU AS AN EFFECTIVE LEADER

Why did you or did you not list yourself as an effective leader?

As your definition of an effective leader continues to unfold and especially as you choose to capture it in words and examples that have meaning to you, let's begin to consider why you want to do this any way!

Chapter 2

MISSION

Why matters

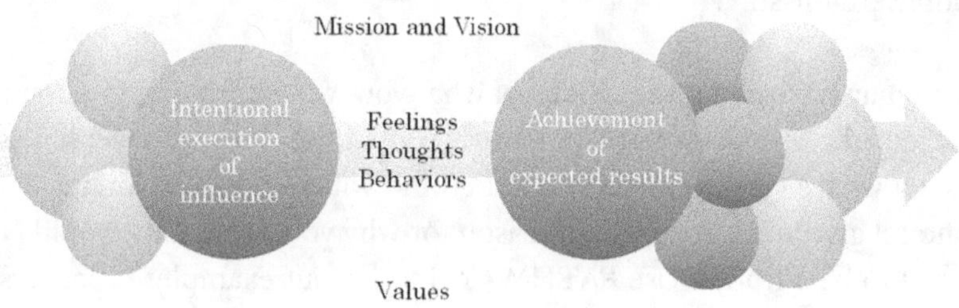

Why are the motives that represent underlying desires that drive, select, and evaluate behaviors we choose that satisfy persistent needs, values, passions, pleasures and purpose. It is why we do what we do.
It is your mission.

Now that you have a personal working definition of effective leadership, a beginning framework for WHAT is effective leadership, let's consider WHY. While you still have a range of choices, the number or reasonable options is reduced when you have a clear sense of mission and vision, and insight regarding your motivators and values. What represents that higher order driver for your choices and sense of satisfaction? What represents those internal drivers that often lie beneath the surface yet serve as powerful activators of your choices, and serve as criteria for your sense of satisfaction?

Let's start with examples of early or vivid memories of you in a leadership role. The first one represents examples of Less Desirable Leadership Moments. These should be instances in which you were in a leadership role and regardless of the results, you were frustrated, confused, anxious, or pretending to be the leader. Think of at least three situations so that you can see a hint of patterns and common themes. What situations come to mind? What led up to you being selected to fill what role? What did you do, what were you thinking, and very importantly, what were you feeling? These Less Desirable Leadership Moments will give some hint as to what you were missing.

You may have had a vague idea of what you were searching for. You may have had a clear idea but was frustrated that the thing you were missing is not where you hoped to find it. Remind yourself of how you reacted. It should give you a compelling reason for why you personally would NOT want to be a leader. Use **PATHWAY 5** to lay out examples of leadership moments that were less desirable for you,

PATHWAY 5: LESS DESIRABLE LEADERSHIP MOMENTS

Describe 2-3 Less Desirable Leadership Moments.

What led up to each situation?

What did you feel, think or do?

What was the outcome in each situation?

Here are a couple of examples of Less Desirable Leadership Situations from my personal experience. One reason they are offered is to invite you to look for examples of leadership situations for you that may have occurred years ago. Some of these remain vivid and impactful for how you define, in this instance, examples of leadership on your part that left a negative impression. What do we learn even from these instances?

PATHWAY 5A: LESS DESIRABLE LEADERSHIP MOMENTS - SAMPLE

Describe 2-3 Less Desirable Leadership Situations.

Situation (1)

- *Summer job to clean up neighborhood streets and playgrounds*

Situation (2)

- *Manager of new consulting organization in training company; Team included current employees with subject matter expertise outside of; people hired by President and assigned to me but managed by President*

What led up to each situation?

- *Supervisor saw me as more mature than others and made me crew leader*
- *Invited to take on role by CEO based on past relationship*

What did you feel, think or do?

- *Tried to be "the boss", issuing ultimatum*
- *Lost emotional control and "hit him"*
- *Frustrated*
- *Focused on "proving" I was adding value*
- *Uncertain about what authority and support I had*

What was the outcome in each situation?

- *Demoted!*
- *Drew's image enhanced and mine diminished*
- *Became transactional in interactions with some direct reports*

Though the first example comes from an early stage of my leadership journey, it is full of lessons learned. Here are more details of the first situation listed.

I could not articulate it at the time but some young kid named Drew gave me a clear, compelling picture of WHY I would NOT want to be a leader. What is funny in hindsight about this event that occurred when I was 13 years old is that everything started out in a relatively positive light. I was just starting my very first official job. It was not lofty but it was "good" work. In the aftermath of riots in Cleveland Ohio, a community agency called Cleveland Pride was formed. One of the many things it did was to give jobs to inner city youth that included cleaning the streets and painting playgrounds in our own neighborhoods. I was surprised, pleased, anxious and proud when the supervisor made me squad leader on the first day! I knew I was one of the most introverted kids in the group, below average in size and perhaps in middle of the age pack. All I had to do was tell the other kids where to sweep the curb and to stay together. Drew decided he didn't have to sweep. He also decided he was not impressed with my soft-spoken logic. He may also have decided since he outweighed me by a few pounds that if he chose to sit on the curb rather than sweep it, then I would not be able to make him. I did not actually have to guess his position on this because he had in fact sat down and emphatically responded to my leader-like order of "Drew you have to sweep!" with his own exclamation of "You can't make me!" I was embarrassed because he challenged my 13-year old authority in ear shot of the rest of my squad, frustrated because I had exhausted the power of my positional power when I said you HAVE to, and angry because I did not have many other options, didn't want the role anyway, and suddenly knew I didn't like him. I did have one or two other options. I went for option one and hit him with the broom. Now Dang Difficult Drew became Big D the Cry-Baby!! (Crying was going to be my other option). How did my first day as an official leader end? My supervisor rescued my "bad employee", chastised me in public and demoted me from street sweeper squad leader. All this for $1.64 an hour.

I remember thinking, why would I want to be a leader? Why would I dare think I would ever be good at it?

Step back from what you have listed and look for patterns, common themes and insights. What are these examples telling you about *your leadership signature*?

PATHWAY 6: LESS DESIRABLE LEADERSHIP MOMENTS INSIGHTS

What are common elements of the situations you chose to describe?

Identify patterns in what led up to the situations.

What was typical in your reactions?

List any similarities in the outcomes.

What do your situations say about your leadership signature?

It took me awhile to admit that there was a different level of insight to be gained from accessing different modes of introspection. I was more inclined to work things out in my head. Even when reading a book like this or pushing through a workbook in a leadership development program, I would typically prefer doing the absorption, analysis, and reflection all in my head. If you looked at my workbooks, you would at best see a few bullet points. I resisted putting things in print. Often my coaching clients showed the same resistance and I imagine many readers will be doing the same as they page through this book.

In the same way saying something out loud brings a different level of clarity to what you are thinking, putting things in print are likely to generate a different level of insight than keeping it all in your head. This is also the reason why I am pushing you and my clients to generate at least three examples of every situation to reveal patterns and to stimulate more insight.

Following and filling out all of the questions in each PATHWAY is not absolutely critical to the process of mapping your journey. Using your reactions to the questions and suggestions is however a valuable source of data for you. In each instance, what is most critical is purposefully paying attention to how everything you feel, think, say and do are clues to defining *your leadership signature*. If you find yourself rushing through this journey, just pause and ask what does this say about you?

Instead of completing **PATHWAY 6** by answering the questions about common elements, patterns, and common threads, I went directly to the question: what do your situations say about *your leadership signature*?

This is how I responded when I stepped back to look at what I wrote and had begun to analyze in my head!

- *Benefit from having to time to prepare for the role rather than unexpectedly getting it*
- *Can be overly concerned about image*
- *Focused on what I thought the role was "supposed" to be*

- *Not as effective when I inherited team members without being able to choose them*
- *Had limited repertoire to influence worker*
- *Formal authority was ineffective*

If you were resisting following each PATHWAY step by step and trying to work it all out in your head, what additional insights did you get when you did put something in print?

The second set of examples to explore are MORE DESIRABLE LEADERSHIP MOMENTS. Don't shy away from the emotional excitement that accompanies the moment you find something that you have been searching for whether you had a clear vision of what it was, or you claimed you would know it once you found it. Joy? Relief? Excitement? It should give you a compelling reason for why you WOULD personally want to be a leader. Similar to PATHWAY 6 think of a few examples of situations that you would consider to be representative of when you had a more desirable leadership moment than average. Enjoy the process of recalling and potentially re-telling these leadership moments.

PATHWAY 7: MORE DESIRABLE LEADERSHIP MOMENTS

Describe 2-3 More Desirable Leadership Moments

Situation (1)

Situation (2)

Situation (3)

What led up to each situation?

What did you feel, think, and do?

What was the outcome in each situation?

Every time I have a client to recall an example of anything, I am intrigued with the process they use to decide how to define the category and how to sort through the number of experiences they have that may or may not qualify. Though I am genuinely interested in the list they eventually share, I am equally intrigued with the sorting and selecting they go through to get there. I remember a leader taking 20 minutes to seek more clarity about what I was asking, and to talk about examples that did not fit before sharing their final choices. Those first 20 minutes offered almost as much insight about their leadership style as did the actual examples they shared.

As many times as I have gone through this exercise myself, I am fascinated with my own reflections about what would represent an example from my own experiences. The examples I quickly sort through change slightly from one iteration to the next. The details I recall and the way I recount them shift some as well. Though I usually convince myself that the broad themes remain consistent, I do learn more about myself and refine my insights each time. The list you see below is my current version of examples of More Desirable Leadership Moments.

Whether your list and insights stay the same from one time doing this to the next, I invite you to share the list with someone else and ask them to answer the last question about you: what do your situations say about *your leadership signature?*

PATHWAY 7A: MORE DESIRABLE LEADERSHIP MOMENTS

Describe 2-3 More Desirable Leadership Moments

Situation (1)
- *Conflict between management and union regarding diversity and inclusion issue*

Situation (2)

- *Persistent errors in production and quality of fuel packages for nuclear plant and increased finger pointing at who was responsible*

Situation (3)

- *Charged with updating global leadership competencies, establishing enterprise framework for succession planning*

What led up to each situation?

- *Invited as consultant from Diversity Training organization*
- *Requested as internal resource with credibility regarding team performance expertise and seen as being even-tempered*
- *Shift from decentralized to enterprise orientation*

What did you feel, think, and do?

- *Facilitated monthly meeting with management reps and union reps; including pre-meetings with leadership from both sides*
- *Valued*
- *Facilitated quarterly meetings presenting minimal content and providing process consulting*
- *Assembled diverse team including deep expertise and foundational skills in stretch assignments and risky levels of responsibility*

What was the outcome in each situation?

- *Partnership among adversaries*
- *Reduction in re-dos, increase in quality*
- *High adoption rate of the leadership expectations model*
- *Increase in utilization of talent review database*
- *Significant career acceleration and elevation*
- *Proud*
- *Effective use of different types of influence*
- *Made a difference by building relationships and taking risks with resources*

What do your situations say about *your leadership signature?*

- *Action verbs of choice: facilitate, coordinate, take the risk of offering stretch assignments*
- *Enjoyed being able to advocate for adversaries*
- *Pleased to connect others as resources*
- *Able to fix problems, smooth processes, increase capability and capacity*
- *Used influence and relationship power*
- *Did what I was passionate about*

Take time now to look at common elements and patterns in your More Desirable

Leadership Moments as you did with the Less Desirable ones. Recognize that it may not be obviously true that a pattern in one is simply the opposite of that pattern in another one. While it is also tempting to suggest that it is natural to want to avoid those situations we consider to be negative, painful, or otherwise less desirable, there may be instances as a leader where we still need to manage the circumstances we inherit. Having a clear sense of how we emotionally respond to these categories of leadership moments, gives us an opportunity to increase our effectiveness by leveraging resources and other skill sets.

Similarly, though I may be clear about what I consider to be more desirable leadership situations and even be intentional about pursuing them, I may not have as much influence as I want to shape those situations to what I most desire. It is also true that I am likely to have to balance what I desire with what the situation needs.

One of the leadership programs I facilitate focuses on getting early career professionals to appreciate their strengths and talents. As a group of high potential individuals selected through a competitive process, they all seemed excited about being encouraged to nurture and leverage their strengths. They participated in a similar exercise of recalling and analyzing situations in which their influence and impact seemed natural and in which they really found enjoyment. It took more effort for them to understand how that same pursuit of desirable leadership moments might contribute to times of over using those strengths. Are there benefits to pursuing what would be the More Desirable Leadership Moments for you? Yes. Are their subtleties in those situations and implications of that pursuit worth introspection and feedback from others? Absolutely.

PATHWAY 8: MORE DESIRABLE LEADERSHIP MOMENTS INSIGHTS

What are common elements of the situations you chose to describe?

Identify patterns in what led up to the situations.

What was typical in your reactions?

List any similarities in the outcomes.

What do your situations say about *your leadership signature*?

Even if you are clear about what you do not want to do, your Less Desirable Leadership Moments, and what you do want to do, your More Desirable Leadership Moments, have you crafted it in written form? Whether you call it a mission statement, purpose statement, credo, manifesto, or personal charter only matters to the degree the words you use lend even more clarity to what you say, more conviction to the commitments implied, and more accountability to the actions and behaviors promised.

I asked Pat, a coaching client, if he had ever crafted a personal mission statement. His answer was no, but he was excited about the prospect of developing one. The timing seemed appropriate as we began our coaching engagement focusing on how he could accelerate and elevate his effectiveness in his current role to become a group President.

His first draft was predictably boring. It was a "one size fits all" replay of what a high potential leader should say. He included **what** he wanted to do, with hints of *how*, but very little flavoring of *why*. I asked, "if I gave this to someone who knew you well and considered you to be an effective leader, would they recognize it as you?" His answer was "no" so we took crafting a mission statement as one of his goals.

Over the years and over the hundreds of leaders with whom I have worked, my guess is that not more than 20% have taken time to write out their personal or professional mission statement. Does it matter?

Why do you make the choices you make? What difference do you make? What consistently brings you a level of focus, excitement, satisfaction, and impact? What is your brand that others will recognize up close and from a distance? What is the fingerprint, the signature, you leave that others will recognize?

I asked Chris to think about examples of when he was so focused on what he was doing that others may have had to tap him on the shoulder to get his attention; so engaged in and excited by his efforts that he lost track of time; so pleased about what he was doing that someone else may have thought he was smiling for no apparent reason; so proud of how what he was doing made a difference in how he and others felt, thought, behaved that he needed no outside reinforcement or reward. I thought he looked at me as though I really was showing my psychology roots! What I realized was that I was in pursuit of my own passion at that moment, trying to make a difference in his development.

Chris admitted that his first draft sounded bland. He began sharing how he really enjoyed wood carving. One's true passion and purpose is more likely rooted deeply in experiences that are outside the context in which we first ask the question. Why wood carving I asked? With a smile, Chris said, "I don't know. There is something about taking a piece of wood and seeing what it can become. Not just watching it take shape but knowing that a chip here, a file there and suddenly you see the piece of wood becoming… more….."

Chris is still working on the wording for his official mission statement. More importantly he is getting more in touch with why he really wants to make a difference, why he gets excited developing direct reports and his team, why he wants to be proud of the organization he builds, why he will smile regardless of what others think.

I took Carolyn through a similar process. Hers quickly moved from a "one mission statement fits anyone" feel to one she saw as proudly reflecting her personally. She told me she had it printed, framed and hanging on the wall in her office. I asked her what happens when people come in and see it? She replied they typically initiate a discussion about it, and all of my direct reports asked: "so can I hold you to that?" She has a clearer picture of why she wants to be a leader. Both she and the members of her team are more likely to hold her accountable.

Do you have a personal or professional mission statement? Is it written? Have you captured your WHY? How have you shared it with others?

If you prefer to have a structure to shape your mission statement, consider the one provided in **PATHWAY 10**. I have offered my personal mission statement in after it. The content, style and tone all feel like me. It is only 76 words, I could read it even with dramatic overplay in about 40 seconds, but if you had the time, I could spend from hours to a whole life time telling you what lies between the lines. I hope you have an obvious glow of pride and passion when you unfold your mission statement. It is clearly an illustration of *your leadership signature!*

As you refine your picture of why want to be a leader, drawing from samples of Less Desirable Leadership Moments and More Desirable Leadership Moments, how do you tap into why you do what you do in general? Many of us open up conversations when we meet others by asking what is it that you do. We often answer in ways that include our titles and sometimes what we do. I am Director of Human Resources. I am responsible for developing and implementing hiring policies. I am a Regional Practice Leader. I lead a team of trainers and we provide consulting and coaching to improve our clients use of its talent. Our responses can be fairly automatic and even predictable.

Imagine someone meeting you and asking: why do you do what you do?

Robert approached me during a break in a leadership development program as we prepared for the next exercise built around your "why". He asked, what if I do not know my why? I offered a temporary suggestion for him to consider when he had choices to make and what influenced those choices. How did you choose among the college choices you had? How did you decide which job opportunity to pursue? What guided your decisions about where you elected to take a stand? What are your non-negotiables? What do you value that you know you are unwilling to compromise? What makes you smile, leaves you feeling pleased and proud?

If we are asked why rather than what, our responses are certainly less automatic. Yet, they are very likely to be far more revealing of who you are as a person. On this journey mapping your leadership signature, your responses are also likely to be more revealing of you as a leader as well. Follow **PATHWAY 9** to describe your why.

PATHWAY 9: WHAT IS YOUR WHY

Instead of "what" you do, describe "why" you do.

Companies and organizations typically have written mission statements and values statements. Leaders in those organizations may have been part of the team that spent the weekend retreat to craft them. How do you come up with a personal mission statement? You may find a template or format that helps you articulate and structure a statement that works for you. As I mentioned earlier regarding my work with Chris, Carolyn, and Robert, the challenge iS crafting a statement that really is your signature.

Use **PATHWAY 10** as example of a format for crafting your Mission Statement. It has been helpful with some clients because it pulled out what we both considered to be a "draft" version. As I mentioned earlier, seeing some things in print can be more revealing than keeping them in your head. Try this approach if you feel stuck, or resistant. The process of thinking it through, deciding what to put in print, which is a version of making it public, and the predictable reaction of embracing, editing, or even dismissing your draft, will constitute at least a few steps along the journey.

PATHWAY 10: MISSION STATEMENT

I am (adjective describing your greatest virtue – e.g. a leader/doer/being who is)

____

____

____

____

____

____

____

____

____

Committed to (statement of your purpose)

____

____

____

____

____

____

By (the actions you take)

And by leveraging my strengths of

I will (action items you take)

To achieve (results)

I had fragments of my mission statement in my head for many years. When I finally pushed to put it in print, I skipped the format approach and began with the question: what am I living for? What you see below is close to the way I first wrote it. The content represents what I believe in and the way it reads also captures my leadership signature in a way that people who know me recognize it as something I would say.

PATHWAY 8A - PENNINGTON MISSION STATEMENT – SAMPLE

I live my life between memories and dreams. Not one over the other but a blend between the two. I look to the past to remember where I am from. I look to the future to remind me I am not yet done. The gifts God gave to me I give to you. I want to lift you up, not let you down. I want to make a difference in what you feel, think, and do.

Greg Pennington

Chapter 3

VISION

How I collect and connect the dots

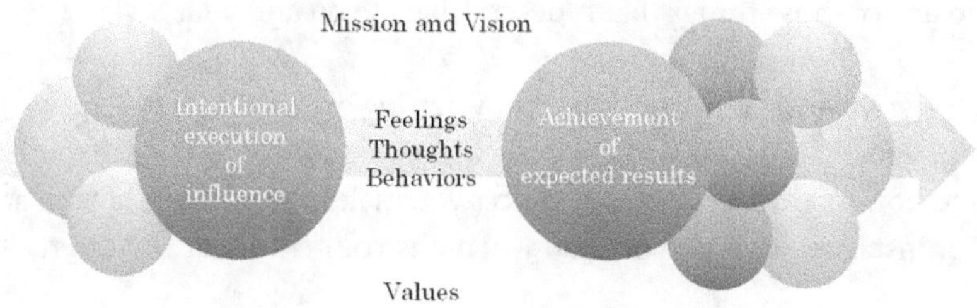

*Leaders need vision, which includes being able to see
what others have yet to see, identifying choices in
goals to pursue and paths to choose, and effectively
convincing others what they should do and why.*

There are several images that come to mind that serve as metaphors for leadership. Traditionally these include military, sports, religious, animals, and birds. I once heard someone use a lifeguard as a metaphor to illustrate a differentiating capability of an effective leader. When I heard this CEO use it, it was in the midst of a changing and challenging business climate. When asked to elaborate he talked about the importance of having a vantage point that provided enough vision to look towards the horizon and to sharply focus on what was beneath your feet. He added not only was it important to be able to read changes on the surface of the water and anticipate what lay below the surface, it was also important to be able to quickly discern the difference between the momentary crisis of a missed stroke and the point of an imminent major disaster.

Some aspect of vision, strategic thinking and decision making, creativity, innovation, learning and agility are likely to be on any list of critical capabilities of an effective leader. After you gain that vantage point of seeing what lies ahead, what is right in front of you and what lies beneath the surface, how do you identify what options you have and how do you choose among them? Perhaps most important in the role of leadership is how do you effectively communicate your vision in a way that results in influencing the way others feel, think and behave? As we continue on this journey of defining *your leadership signature*, what is it about the way you do any of those things that is descriptive of you and your style?

One way we expand our vision is by getting exposed to new experiences and information. With an almost endless possibility of what to experience and how to experience it, the choices you make are reflective of your style. For instance, what do you read when it is your choice of what to read?

One component of most talent management processes is a regular discussion among a small group of people about a short list of key leaders. Some of the questions raised are fairly routine and predictable. A CEO with whom I worked always asked a particular question that had a significant impact on the discussion: What does this person read? What fascinated me about the question was it reminded me of a quote I heard somewhere: "not all readers are leaders, but all leaders should be readers."

What does what you read suggest about you? Reading historical biographies for instance is an interesting way to get a glimpse of how leaders felt, thought, and reacted to challenges and opportunities in the context of their times and their business climate. You can also certainly make literal inferences about what a person is interested in and what insights they are seeking as well as their overall interest in learning.

More to the point, reading does three critical things for your success as a leader and defining *your leadership signature*. It builds your vision, emotional intelligence, and options for execution.

In regards to vision, reading enhances your overall strategic thinking by accumulating more information and more diverse perspectives. This was an argument one business President raised when they insisted on requiring candidates for a particular role have MBA degrees. When I pushed for what they assumed the Masters in Business Administration guaranteed, they talked about the expectation that the candidate would have been exposed to a wide range of business cases and studies that contributed to their overall capability to see patterns in data, to analyze choices and consequences, and to build a frame of reference for solving problems. Accumulating data points seems essential. How you gather those points contributes to defining you as a leader.

When I decided to move from a likely traditional career as a Clinical Psychologist into leadership consulting, I asked someone with a similar background and already in the field for suggestions. They asked what business publications I read on a regular basis. They clearly saw through my muddled attempt to describe some low level of exposure to this genre, because they pointedly told me to take out a few subscriptions, read them for at least three months and come back to them then. Since then I have steadily accessed sources of reading I have reason to believe most leaders read. I came to presume that all leaders were active readers. However, it has been my experience that some leaders read very little. Others confess they only read what is necessary and may only access one or two sources of information.

Vision also includes understanding and influencing yourself and others, emotional intelligence. Though there are variations in how emotional intelligence is defined and measured, the core elements include how well do you know yourself, how well do you know others, and how well do you leverage that knowledge to achieve intended results. Reading is one source of information about how others feel, think and behave. It is also a way to exercise our own thoughts and emotions we may not express during our day to day routines. This is particularly true when your source is an autobiography or a first-person account of leadership moments. What were people feeling, thinking, and doing when they came up with that analysis of the situation? Did they know how others would react when presented with those options? What have others done to manage their frustrations and excitement?

Vision also involves anticipating the impact of decisions that are executed. Reading can expand your repertoire of, if not "best practices", at least reference points for how others addressed situations. The most direct example of this relative to leadership in organizations is accessing business case stories and articles in business focused publications.

So, what have you been reading this year, what insights have you gained, and what does your list suggest about *your leadership signature?*

Use **PATHWAY 11** to list recent books you have read as well as books your frequently reference.

PATHWAY 11: LEADERS AS READERS

What books have you read in the past year?

What books have you frequently quoted over the past year?

What common themes are apparent in the books you have read and frequently quote?

There are seven books on my shelf now where I place my active reading for professional purposes. In my casual room there are 3 other books and beside the bed are two others. Among the collection are books about a favorite football team, the founder of Judo, a fantasy fictional world written by someone reviewed as one of the next great authors, three leadership books offered me by a client, one by an applied psychologist, another one on executive coaching, two on transformational change, and one recently published, cutting edge book on race, gender and leadership.

Often when I asked this question of clients, the response is "I usually just read technical stuff and things related to work. I know I should probably read more". I did not realize until I inventoried my own list that I actually read more for work than pleasure as well. I also have books that are more reactive to specific suggestions from others, including clients, than I have ones that were gathered because of something I anticipated on my own. As much as I think I use creative metaphors in my leadership style, I am not actively accumulating a diverse range of sources for metaphors. The judo book works well as a source of metaphors, but I am not sure reading about the history of the golden era of an underperforming professional football team is expanding my repertoire in a helpful way!

I actually read a lot each day from a variety of sources. More accurately, I scan a lot each day from a variety of sources that include sources with different perspectives from mine. What does it say about my leadership signature regarding vision? I want to know a little bit about a lot of things. I want to use those points of information and perspectives to inform my hypotheses about what may be going on and what are possibilities for connecting ideas and testing explanations. I use them to help me see the beginnings of possibilities. It is a very different approach to collecting the dots than those who want to intentionally go deeper on a few things rather than wide on many.

Back to your reading list and taking the next step in PATHWAY 11, what does your list say about the way you collect information?

I used reading as one example of how you gather information that reflects *your leadership signature.* Most of the same questions and insights can be applied to what persons do you consider credible reference points and active thought partners. Who have you leveraged as a source of information and intellectual stimulation over the past six months?

You have accumulated data points. You recognize patterns, possibilities and probabilities. You have choices to make with consequences and contingencies to consider.

Some leaders are influenced and seek to influence others through logic. The signature approach of others is ultimately based on personal experiences and evidence of what predecessors and other credible reference points have done. Another style relies more on intuition and another's choices are made by the excitement the choice generates in them. You can find studies that suggest what percentage of leaders fall into what categories in their approach to making decisions. The journey here is to define what is *your leadership signature.*

Let's assume one goal in sorting through options is to identify at least three choices for how to move forward developing a strategy, generating next steps and action plans, what is the approach you take to make these choices? Are you the one driven by logic and thorough analysis? Are you the one defined by intuition? Are you calculating probabilities for success and weighing known and unknown risk factors? Are you willing to fail or to succeed?

When you have three reasonably comparable options, how do you determine which one to take? On the surface your decisions may appear to be influenced by analytics including return on investments, or a risk/benefits analysis. They are also a rich source of indicators about *your leadership signature.* Think of several recent examples of dilemmas you faced. Consider a dilemma a situation in which you have two or more choices of which none are obviously better than the others.

Think of three examples of dilemmas, one involving personal decisions, one related to choices involving direct reports, and a third one concerned with decisions related to your team. For example, a personal dilemma may have been when you had to decide where to go to college, which job offer to accept, whether to confront your manager or a peer to decide whether to tell or not to tell them how their behavior affected you. A direct report dilemma may have been when you had options of giving an employee more time to complete a project, in support of their development or to reassign it to someone else to assure it was done. A dilemma involving your team might be an instance when you had to choose how to restructure the group and assign roles and responsibilities. PATHWAY 12 offers a framework for considering how you make decisions when you have several available and viable options.

PATHWAY 12: CHOICES AND DECISIONS

Describe 1-2 examples of a *personal* dilemma.

List three options you had to resolve the dilemma.

What decision criteria did you use to make your choice?

Describe 1-2 examples of a *direct report or peer* **dilemma.**

List three options you to resolve the dilemma.

What decision criteria did you use to make your choice?

Describe 1-2 examples of a *leadership team* dilemma.

List three options you had to resolve the dilemma.

What decision criteria did you use to make your choice?

What themes are common in all three types of dilemmas?

What stands out to you regarding your approach to making choices?

Vision is part of *your leadership signature*. Gathering information to see patterns and possibilities is one part of vision. Your approach to making choices is another part. Communicating in a way that impacts others as intended and in a way that is genuine and authentic is a third component of vision. Does it sound like something you would say?

I was asked to prepare talking points for our CEO. I had not claimed to be a speech writer but I did believe I could capture key talking points and even suggest how to frame them, where to place them, how to enrich them with metaphors and transitions, and how I imagined I could capture the passion of the point that not only felt like the CEO had written it himself but would also result in the audience being inspired. The CEO gracefully said, "thank you. I have it from here."

What is your signature way of communicating with others? Are you an inspiring visionary? An encouraging reinforcer? A constant critic with feedback and redirection? You may have an intuitive sense of what sounds like you. Making that sense of yourself conscious and intentional increases the probability of repeating that communication style and purposefully increasing its effectiveness.

If you have not recently recorded yourself, that would be an important initial step. One obvious exercise is to record yourself and view it looking for behavioral tendencies, repetitive words, non-verbal fillers, metaphors, and behavioral tics. My wife claims I use the word "basically" too often. I notice I clear my throat frequently. A client called me Socrates because I constantly said, "it's like…". I recognize that I am inclined to integrate metaphors related to my personal passions – art, dance, judo, and I still have hyper-active hands!!!

Your video recording will provide you with strong points to leverage and distracting elements worth addressing. It will also literally give you a picture of what you look like and sound like. If you were producing a video of you at your best, capturing *your leadership signature* in terms of how you communicate a vision, how you deliver encouraging feedback and recognition, how to manage critical, constructive, corrective feedback, there it is!

Assemble your highlight reel. Listen to it with the sound on. Look at it with the sound off. If you have the luxury of enlisting an insightful writer, ask them to write a short speech for you. Whatever the content is ask them to make sure it reads like something you would say and encourage them to include any catch phrases you are "known" to use.

PATHWAY 13: COMMUNICATION STYLE

What do others say sounds like what you would say?

What do you agree or disagree with?

What are common themes in what others say sounds like you?

What does your communication style indicate about *your leadership signature*?

I asked my direct reports to generate a list of things that sounded like what I would say. They generated a long page of Penn-isms! Most of which I agreed with right away and would gladly claim. A few left me wondering had they confused me with a former boss. I also asked them what would a non-verbal video of me include. They nailed it. The exercise was also a powerful way of capturing what I was doing especially non-verbally that contributed to others recognizing me and mis-reading me. When I looked for themes in what they shared I saw how long my communications typically were (get to the point!), how complex I often made them, how frequently I referenced other sources for credibility, and how often I integrated personal stories. My signature insights included how much my style was reflected in painting a picture with words, and working to connect my message to personal experiences and perspectives, grounding it in practical ways and wrapping it in logic. (See what I mean about being wordy?)

Chapter 4

IMPACT

What buttons I push driving for results

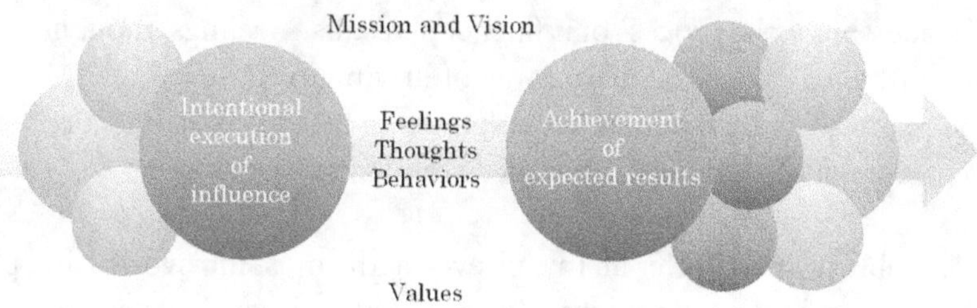

Leadership involves influencing others to achieve results and demonstrating agility to adjust to situations and individuals.

I was asked what was the one critical component in being an effective leader. I suggested that a leader needed to understand and leverage their power. One critical component in a definition of effective leadership is the delivery of results. In some situations, results seem to be the only thing that matter. Certainly, there are leaders and leadership styles that have a dimension of power that can be used to force, compel, or require others to do what is ordered or commanded. Some leaders actually recognize that in themselves and willingly claim that as their signature style of leadership. It may also be true that some leaders are not aware that their behaviors are experienced by others in that way.

Do you have a need for power? I have asked that to a number of audiences in leadership development programs over the years. Few people raise their hands or otherwise respond in the affirmative. That includes me. When the question is changed to how many of you have a need for influence, many more have exhaled and said "Oh if you put it that way, yes!"

There are instances in which the situation and perhaps the organization sets an expectation that how one drives for results is as important as simply achieving results. Despite how some may react to describing one aspect of their motivation to be a leader as a need for power, it is important to understand where your source of power – influence – comes from.

If leadership is the process of influencing results – feelings, thoughts, and actions, what is your signature way of driving to those results? More to the point, where is your source of power to influence the reactions and behaviors of others that lead to those results?

I probably wanted power all my life even at the most introverted and passive stages of my development. My mother always admonished me to not think I was better than anyone else. I held myself in check because I did not want to upstage others, be accused of always wanting to be the one in control, acting like I was the boss, coming across as though I was the one with all the answers. The truth is and perhaps has always been that I do think I am better at some things than some people, I actually do want to step upstage from others when the moment calls for it, I will take control when I think I am adding value, I do not mind being the boss when I can do it in a way that fits me and I am making a difference, and I do think I have some of the answers. The challenge is not what do I want to do. It is how can I influence others and learn while leading.

What do you use to lead? What is your source of power? I know there are numerous models describing power in the context of leadership. Two particular models helped me articulate what I saw as sources of influence in leaders and directly impacted how I have come to understand my own approach to leadership. French and Raven's classic work on five bases power and Raven's addition of a sixth base is one of those models. David

McClelland's distinction between need for personal power and need for social power is the second one.

As you read the simple outline below of French and Raven's sources of power, look at them in the context of three recent examples of what you relied on to influence the feelings, thoughts and behaviors of others. Plan to capture your reflections about how you might have used that particular source of power in the three examples you recalled. Keeping in mind that this is an exercise to help you identify and refine your personal leadership signature, look for and prepare to capture insights about what you consider to be the most accurate way to describe how you mix and blend these sources of power.

SOURCE OF POWER	DEFINITION
Legitimate	Formal authority associated with title and expectation of others to comply
Reward	Ability to provide or withhold recognition including compensation
Expert	Leverage of credible high levels of skill and expertise
Referent	Perceived attractiveness and positive affiliations
Coercive	Ability to punish others for non-compliance
Information	Control of information needed by others to accomplish their goals

Adapted from Bertram Raven, "The Bases of Power and the Power/Interaction Model of Interpersonal Influence," *Analyses of Social Issues and Public Policy,* Vol. 8, no. 1, 2008, pp.1-22

It is important to think of enough examples to suggest a pattern of your behavior. It is also important to recall examples that are fairly recent so that you are more likely to accurately recall the details of what you felt, said and did. There is no absolute time parameter to define "fairly recent". Usually when working with leaders I ask them to consider examples in the last five years. Often times there is a compelling reason to recapture an example beyond that time frame when it represents a significant chapter in that person's development as a leader. The key to this exercise is to gather examples that are vivid and to assemble enough of them to suggest a pattern.

Sometimes I have introduced the exercise as "suppose we are to make a documentary video of you as a leader. If I had been able to observe you in a situation of you influencing others, what would I see?"

Ready to outline your video documentaries of "You-In the exercise of power!"?

PATHWAY 14: SOURCES OF POWER

List 2-3 examples of when you said or did something to intentionally influence the behavior of others to achieve a specific result.

Describe what led up to each situation.

What were you feeling or thinking as you considered how to influence the individuals involved and the outcomes?

What was the outcome? Consider how the other persons felt and what they thought in reaction to what you did.

How would you describe the sources of power you used?

Each time I review my leadership videos, I recognize that I am most consistently drawing on a combination of Referent and Expert sources of power. I leverage relationships that are most often built on initial attractions to each other in terms of similarities and a range of affiliations and natural connections. I have grown more intentional in leveraging this source by actively looking for points of connection that would enhance the attraction between me and others I am seeking to influence. I also recognize that I am inclined to take advantage of a position of expertise as a source of influence. I admit that I have chided a colleague, who also has a doctorate in psychology, for often seizing a moment of influence by opening his comments with "the research says…"

My examples of sources of influence include one in the early but vivid category. It has proven helpful to me in understanding my style because it reminds me that while I may assess my behaviors based on my intentions, others will undoubtedly assess my behaviors on what I actually did and how it made them feel and think. As you see in the example that follows, Jane would more likely describe me as using the Legitimate power of my role, or the implied Coercive power of my role than any of the other choices.

In my first internal corporate role as Director of Human Resources I underestimated the impact of legitimate power while trying to exercise referent power. I encouraged Jane, a mortgage processor, to apply for a loan officer role soon to be posted in another branch. She listened and went directly to her manager and asked if there was something he had not told her about her job stability. She interpreted my mention of another job as a warning that, her job was in jeopardy since she heard me speaking from my HR position. The use of legitimate power is not my strong suit.

Even when I recognize the impact of being an expert, I recognize that my base of knowledge is usually more broad than deep. I typically ask more questions than provide answers. Even when in a more direct advising role, I work to be implicitly or explicitly invited to offer advice. I am most effective and most likely to be effective when I have established a personal connection and relationship. Accompanying this over time is gaining clarity about where, how and with whom am I most likely to connect. Regrettably there are still a few people who do not seem to see from the outset what a nice person I am!

Hopefully you generated ample and detailed footage in your sources of power examples above. You are likely to gain more insight about your patterns when you see those examples in written form than when you just think them through. A follow-up step would be for you to share them with someone else and ask them to describe your source of power.

When I was first introduced to the need for power in a David McClelland classroom it was in the context of learning about key motives that drove behavior. We focused on the needs for Affiliation, Achievement, and Power. After being given the definitions, we were invited to reflect on which of them seemed most descriptive of us. I assumed I would have a profile that showed a stronger drive for Achievement, since I was pretty good at setting realistic and challenging goals. I thought my next strongest driver would be Affiliation because I certainly put some intentional effort in building and sustaining relationships. Power was the third one on my list because I did not see myself as competitive or manipulative. As you may have guessed by now, the need for Power was the strongest for me with drives for Achievement and Affiliation being close to equal. I recall initially rejecting the assessment but gained more self- insight when I stepped back to look at examples of what I actually did, and listened to feedback from others about how my behaviors were interpreted. It also helped to appreciate that for some, the exercise of personal power was driven to satisfy more of their own needs. For others the exercise of social power was closer to influence and driven more to satisfy needs of others than one self. In self-reflection and in coaching others, I often distinguish between these two by asking: are you trying to prove something or to improve something?

Are you driven more by a need for achievement, a need for affiliation, or a need for power (influence)? If you are not sure, who can provide you with a credible source of feedback about what you do, how you do it, and what impact it has on others and the task at hand? And if you weigh in right away with a definitive answer about your drivers and your source of power, who can confirm it?

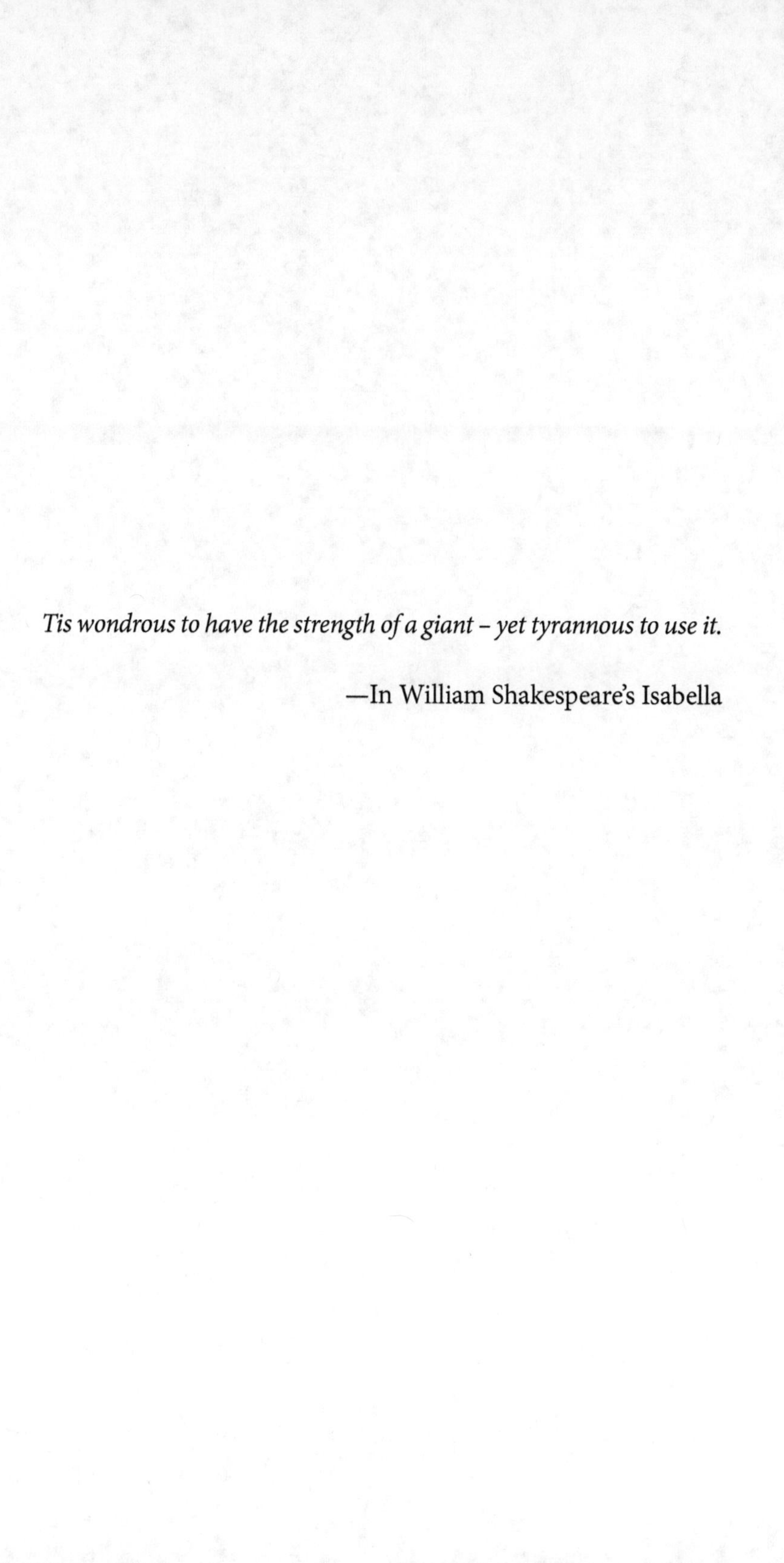

Tis wondrous to have the strength of a giant – yet tyrannous to use it.

—In William Shakespeare's Isabella

Chapter 5

CAPABILITY

Getting more from more

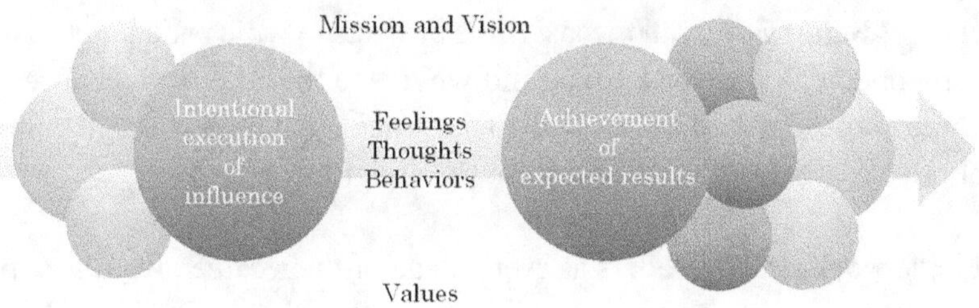

Leaders are challenged to fully leverage all of their people resources. They drive to increase efficiency and effectiveness by enabling each member of their team to make their highest and best contribution each day.

I grew up as an introvert. I was comfortable watching people, imagining what they were thinking, what they had been doing, or planning to do. It was scary at times because reading them meant I was close to what they were feeling, close to understanding what they were thinking, what they had done or were likely to do. A vivid memory of this realization for me came in an emotional conversation with a friend Paul as we reacted to what another person had done. The question tossed before us was simply: "What would possess him to do such an irrational thing!?!" I, coincidentally with my psychology background fully engaged, offered a few hypotheses. Peter, coincidentally with his legal background fully engaged, got stuck on" it doesn't make sense!"

Regardless of education background, some get stuck on "I can't imagine!" If you are to be an effective leader, I am convinced you have to be able to see from another person's perspective, be able to "imagine" what motivates them. This is an important element of emotional intelligence which can be more of a differentiator between less effective and more effective leaders than intellect and experience. The more I can imagine and understand what motivates another person, the more options I have for influencing them.

Imagine you have an important project and need to choose someone on your team to lead it. Who immediately comes to mind as your preferred choice? Better yet, recall the last three projects to which you had to assign someone, who did you choose and why? Are there patterns that readily come to mind regarding your go-to persons? What have you said out loud about why that person would want the assignment?

I have worked with leaders at every stage of their career, from first time supervisor to senior executive, who have struggled with when and how to delegate to others. In addition to asking them who they typically chose and why, I usually asked them to compare and contrast their other options. With any of the situations you recalled above where you chose to assign a project lead role to someone, what if you had to rank order your choices with a rationale for what they could do, how they would do it, what support they would need, and why they would do it, what would your list look like?

Jonathan said one of his challenges was to lead a newly inherited team to high performing levels as they worked to move from a product centered approach to a more solution driven one. He felt limited in his options because he felt he had been given a team of what he described as C-level players. Jonathan's signature leadership style at the time was one who could come into an underperforming situation and turn the team around. He was accustomed to exercising the option of bringing in a few all-stars and often with support for totally re-organizing his team. When I worked with him, he was told to make it work with the team he had inherited. The challenge: how do you get more from more even when you think your players are all C-level?

As you focus on this journey to defining *your leadership signature*, what does it take to intentionally adjust some aspects of your style? Jonathan needed to first recognize and accept that he had some usual tendencies in his approach to getting the most out of others – he went to those with the most obvious skills to get the highest probability of achieving some measurable results. You will get a glimpse of your tendencies when you look at those recent assignments of project roles. Try doing what I asked Jonathan to do in a more structured assessment of your team members current abilities, possible capabilities and your options for getting the most out of them. Remember to calibrate your assessments against the reactions of someone else with whom you share your prioritized list of "usual suspects".

There was another insight to come out of my work with Jonathan, that I will phrase as a question for you: how likely are you to delegate for development compared to delegate for delivery?

My team took on responsibility for an enterprise wide change that involved a high level of visibility across the businesses. It would need a significant amount of input from Group Presidents and required collaboration with sometimes competing business level organizations. I chose a relatively new team member to coordinate the project. My manager's initial reaction was to question my decision and caution me about the risks I was taking. My boss concluded by volunteering they would not make the same choice. To their credit, they insisted the final decision was up to me. This was clearly a moment of delegating for development more than delegating for delivery.

How have you decided when and how to take the risk of giving others stretch assignments? How do you know the person is ready, willing, and able to accept it? What probability of success do you need to take the risk?

Before I ask you to work through **PATHWAY 15** to consider what motivates your current team members, I also want you to consider where does a leader add their highest value in terms of developing the capability of others.

I remember a conversation with Jeff about the role of a leader in getting the most out of his team's performance. He lamented that he spent most of his time working with under-performers and high performers. The time directed toward getting under-performers on track with candid feedback, difficult conversations, and performance improvement plans was disproportionate to the return he was likely to get on his investment of time and support for them. He felt that the time he spent with high-performers was significant as well, supporting them, advocating for them, developing them. I asked him what would they do if he did nothing as their leader. Jeff cocked his head to the side for a second, smiled and said "well the under-performers are likely to regress to their usual minimal level of performance, and the high-performers might actually get to an even higher level!" Before I could respond, Jeff volunteered that the real privilege of leadership is to inspire that middle group of performers, the undecided, to a higher level of performance.

Jeff's insights reminded me that our leadership signature may include being able to get the most out of under-performers, getting high performers to accelerate faster and elevate higher, or being able to uncover talent that resides in some middle category as defined by themselves or defined by the organization. When you complete **PATHWAY 15**, be aware of whether you are more inclined to work with one category of performers more than another.

PATHWAY 15: TEAM CAPABILITY

List your current team members and what motivates them?

Are there patterns in how you describe what motivates your team members?

____

____

____

____

____

____

What effort do you exert to influence/leverage them?

____

____

____

____

____

____

____

____

____

____

____

____

____

List insights from listing the range of options you tend to exercise.

Are there options you believe you are unwilling to do

What insights occur to you when you review the range of options you use to influence your team members?

Let me share with you how I worked through this PATHWAY.

PATHWAY 15A:

List your current team members and what motivates them? (Pathway 12: What drives your team?)

- *Mike – Owning something with status and key stakeholder relationships*
- *Eliza – Being anchored in a structured role and clear deliverables*
- *Stephanie – Enjoyed having stretch assignments and full plate, and being able to leverage relationship building skills*
- *John – Being respected as an expert, and having vehicle to drive personal passions*
- *Ann – Wanted to be seen as subject matter expert and have roles measured objectively*

Are there patterns in how you describe what motivates your team members?

- *Status is one key theme*
- *Working to get right balance between structure and open*
- *Usually trying to position people based on skills in building and leveraging relationships*

What effort do you exert to influence/leverage them?

- *Minimum effort but willingness on my part to trust they will stay aligned, convince them of need to be both practical and creative*
- *Minimal effort, careful balancing respect for their experience and pushing them to try something different, acceptance of different communication style and social energy*
- *Significant effort to maintain constructive confrontation, had to be credibility educated on the details, and appeal to underlying logic and overriding values*

Insights from listing the range of options you tend to exercise

- *Used options of delegation for delivery and delegation for development*
- *Leveraged personal connections and mutual trust*

Are there options you believe you are unwilling to do

- *Did not want to consider having to be directly involved in details*
- *Unwilling to set up expectations that were only measured by objective outcomes*

What insights occur to you when you review the range of options you use to influence your team members?

- *Preferred trusting others to deliver with minimal guidance based on agreed upon overall goals and underlying logic*
- *Wanted team members who valued a significant level of interactions*

How do you get more from more? How do we get the most of others? Often people respond by embracing the Golden Rule: to do unto others as you would have them do unto you. While well-intended, there are limitations to this approach. Implicit in the Golden Rule is what has worked for you is likely to work for others. I prefer you do unto me by giving me the big picture of where we are headed and then allowing me to get there as I choose as long as I am directionally correct. You may prefer I do unto you by giving you a detailed set of steps, project planned with critical milestones, and scheduled updates. Brian insisted that he grew up professionally with bosses who gave him "brutally honest feedback along the way" and expected that others would appreciate it as well. I am a bit more subtle than that so it would be difficult for Brian to get the most out of me by hitting me between the eyes with "brutal feedback".

As we increase diversity and commit to fully leveraging the diversity of all our resources, we will encounter more complexity. The simple truth of people looking to find the best and highest use of their strengths and talents, pushes the expectations for effective leadership. *Your leadership signature* will be challenged to find ways to understand others. This should include your C-players, your under-performers, over-looked performers, and high-performers.

Chapter 6

LEGACY

What difference did I make to whom

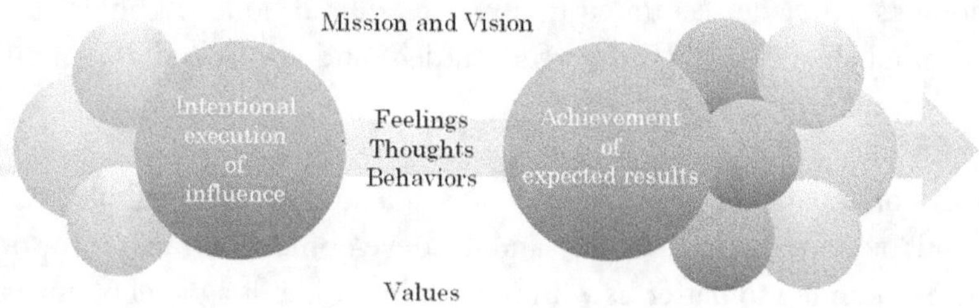

A leader has followers until they pass the torch and get to watch from behind

I started my consulting career with a company focused on process improvements that yielded significant measurable increases in efficiency, effectiveness and profitability. As part of the needs assessment team, we gathered as much data as we could and worked to assemble it in a way to make a compelling story to the senior leader about the need for change and the value we could provide in facilitating that change. The process was tightly managed in a way that included sharing some of the data on Friday, and holding the most revealing information until Monday afternoon. It was not apparent to me why we would hold off some of the information over the weekend. My manager said "every leader is looking for a place and a way to leave their scent. We tell them Friday that something is not working. They spend the weekend getting upset but also planning how to address it. Monday we tell them the rest of the story, and make it more personal about what is happening on their watch. Their legacy is what it important to them." Though the process we used seemed manipulative, what stuck with me was the premise that leaders are looking for places and ways to leave their scent.

More recently a participant in a leadership development program named Steve shared with a group of peers how he had taken time years ago to map out his life in terms of goals. They included where he would go to school, what types of jobs he would have, at what rate he would progress through organizations, what production levels he would achieve and how much money he would make. He included many personal goals and even hobbies. After he recounted them in detail and hollowly noted he had accomplished them all, he tearfully added "and I don't know what difference at all it made".

I was on a panel of "seasoned" leaders at a conference assembled to talk about our careers in leadership and the development of leaders. The organizer intended to flatter us with respect by calling it a panel of gurus. In another instance we were called elders. The assumption was that over the years and after the bumps and bruises, highlights and lowlights, and ideally the wisdom that comes from insight and backward reflection, we could provide some guidance and preview of what the younger audience might anticipate and navigate. Most of the questions were predictable and most of our responses were as well. This was true up until the point when Kevin asked the question: "what does it mean to have lived?"

My contribution was to say that "to have lived means to have made a difference". It was a genuine response but still left me feeling as though I had left something uncaptured and unspoken. Afterwards, I thought my answer should have been: "to have lived means that I would be remembered". There are cultures and philosophies around the world that assert that as long as your name is spoken you will be remembered. What does it mean to have lived? Would that be true about you as a leader? What does it mean to have led?

I ran into Clay after losing contact for several years. We had only worked together briefly and were both generally happy to at least briefly reconnect.

After a few typical pleasantries, he squeezed my hand and said: "you probably don't remember telling me this…" (I held onto my smile but was keenly aware of holding my breath and hoping that he was recalling something pleasant and that I would at least vaguely remember it. He continued: "you told me that if I didn't figure out how to slow down or when to back off, I was going to burn out or blow up! I can't tell you how much that helped me". I just smiled and shared how much I appreciated hearing it, how I learned by sharing and how much I got from giving.

Bob, Victoria, Carolyn and Richard offered a similar affirmation about how I had questioned, focused and restored a team of professionals to get back on track after a period of dysfunction. I was intentional about what difference I wanted to make, what steps I would take to move in that direction, what roles I encouraged others to fill, how I would position potential adversaries to collaborate like allies. Yet, it did not seem like real, sustainable progress until I heard it – unsolicited-from others.

Stacie added another perspective from someone outside of my team. Years after leaving a company where we had both worked and in the early stage of a senior officer role, she called and said: "do you remember the leadership expectations model you built? – (I did.) – I still refer to them today and want to find a way to build them into my new company".

What does it mean to have lived? What does it mean to have led? Who will share "I remember when" stories about you? Who will proudly share how you influenced them, left your fingerprints on them, call you mentor to your surprise? What team will recall the one you led as an example of a high performing team? What did you leave behind for which you were proud? What continues to be remembered and have an impact long after you have gone? What seed did you design, create, install in one setting will someone take to pollinate other outcomes in other settings?

Along this path of intentionally shaping *your leadership signature*, if your legacy is something best told by others, what can you do to intentionally add your signature to it?

Let's begin first by capturing what is already being said about you.

Think back at least 5 years ago but no longer than 10. Recall the people who worked for you in a specific period of time. Also consider peers with whom you worked on a team you led but over whom you had no formal authority. What was the team you led and who was on it? If you remember you had a specific number of direct reports, how many of them can you recall by name? How many of those project team members do you remember? Imagine someone had an opportunity to ask your former direct reports from 5 to 10 years ago to describe you as a leader. What would they recall that stood out about you as a leader, what impact did you have on them? What would they say?

As you work through **PATHWAY 16** that follows, make your own interpretations about what it means that you remember those team members or not after 5-10 years. Generate a few hypotheses about your ability to answer what they are likely to say about you if asked. Then step back to uncover the patterns and themes revealed when you read aloud what you listed as things they would say. This is one view of the legacy of your leadership.

PATHWAY 16: WHAT OTHERS SAY AND REMEMBER ABOUT YOU

List *direct reports and peers* **you have had in last few years.**

What would they say about you if asked?

List 2-3 *teams* you led or were a member of recently.

How would others describe your team? What was your team known for?

Describe 2-3 team accomplishments you of which you are proud.

How have those accomplishments expanded or been sustained over time?

What story unfolds that answers the question of what you are known for and remembered for?

How many of those direct reports and peers did you remember? When was the last time you had any contact with them? Do you know where they are now? Are you proud of them? Are they proud of you?

It did not take much for me to recall the members of my direct teams through the past 10 years. I was more anxious attempting to capture what I thought they would say about me if asked. I took the risk of asking a few of them directly and was pleased to find that I was at least generally aligned with what they said. This included getting feedback from a couple who I had reason to believe were not as likely to place me on their list of examples of an effective leader.

If you have the luxury to do so and willing to take the risk to do so, it would be extremely valuable for you to imagine what 2-3 former team members of yours would say if asked what they remember about you. It is certainly beneficial to ask those who are clearly in your fan club what they would say. It is also beneficial to find a way to get candid feedback from those who were less positive in their reactions to you. In my example that follows I quickly came up with what I thought two former team members might say about me that was not overly positive. I recognize that I had probably already sanitized their reactions and put effort into applying at least a neutral spin on what I thought they would say. Then I allowed myself to imagine that someone might have actually asked them what they thought and they might even somehow come across my version of what I thought they would say! That alone made me push myself to be even more candid in my reflections and insight. It also pushed me to reach out to them and ask.

PATHWAY 2: WHAT OTHERS SAY AND REMEMBER - SAMPLE LIST DIRECT REPORTS YOU HAVE HAD OVER THE PAST FEW YEARS.

- *Sandra*
- *Steve*
- *Michelle*
- *Anna*
- *Barbara*
- *Rochelle*
- *Mike*
- *Adrienne*

What would they say about you if asked?

- *My mentor, took a chance on me moving from role where I was underutilized and put me in one to stretch me*
- *Supported me in a role where he had little expertise, advocated for me without getting in my way*
- *Positioned me where I could add value with little oversight, but seemed to feel threatened*
- *Did not trust me to do more, listened but did not really seem to get it, turned out to be a better peer than boss*
- *Let me challenge him and was able to constructively challenge me, put me in a lead role after being stuck in a support one*
- *Encouraged me to get better at what I was passionate about and prodded me to think of how to get ready for the next level*
- *Let me do my thing but looked for ways to do a little more and to think more broadly*
- *Filled my plate with variety I wanted and pushed me to do more for my career and not just for current role*

List 2-3 teams you led or were a member of in past 5-7 years.

- *Senior leadership development*
- *Regional Practice Leader*
- *Corporate project design team for team coaching*

How would others describe your team? What was your team known for?

- *Combination of subject matter experts and tactical implementers with extensive internal and external networks; relationship builders and collaborators; challenged to build and maintain enterprises standards with adaptability across businesses*
- *Strategic and operational capability; subject matter experts, theoretical and practical; hands-on*
- *Cutting edge designers with practical application; leveraging diverse perspectives*

Describe 2-3 leadership accomplishments in the few years of which you are proud.

- *Revision of enterprise leadership model*
- *Development of enterprise framework for strategic talent reviews*
- *Maintenance of corporate high potential program and use of data to anticipate next phase of revisions*

How have those accomplishments expanded or been sustained since then?

- *Integrated throughout enterprise, High visibility from orientation throughout employee lifecycle*
- *Established senior talent as enterprise resource*
- *Program and its derivatives still active years later*

What story unfolds that answers the question of what you are known for and remembered for?

- *Connected on personal level, advocated for stretch opportunities*
- *Positioned many for expanded roles*

- *More hands off than hands on*
- *Charisma*
- *Worked to balance theoretical and practical*
- *More collaborative than confrontational*
- *Willing to take what is in place and refine*

I remember most of the people who worked for me and many of those with whom I worked over the years. My memory is clearest about those with whom I had a favorable relationship. I can recall specific things people said about me, much of which was said directly to me. From them, I know I am remembered more for how I make others feel than I am for what I did or produced. I am remembered for and known for stimulating the thinking of others, for getting others to collaborate, and for connecting with others. A peer said there is something about the way you connect with others and make them feel listened to. I thanked him and asked what is it that I do? He said you look me in the eye, you listen, and somehow you ask the one question that makes me think differently. I just smiled.

It has been clear to me that we can be intentional developing our leadership signature in how we define leadership, why it matters to us, how we drive for results, how we see and share our vision, and how we build capability and capacity. If, however, our legacy, the fingerprints we leave, is a critical ingredient to effective leadership, and it is essentially defined by what others remember and say about us, how can we intentionally influence their memories and how they describe us to others?

Part of the answer is in your mission statement. Whether offered explicitly or implicitly, when we share our mission statement with others we are sharing our intentions, inviting others to hold us accountable, and suggesting how to remember us. This goes beyond sales numbers and other quantifiable metrics.

I was introduced at a recent speaking engagement by someone who began reading from my bio. I became conscious that I was probably pantomiming the words they were saying since I had written them and had heard them before. I wondered whether the audience was getting as bored as I was. Once the person looked up from their notes and told a personal story about how we had met, and what impact I had on them, my tear ducts got engaged and I sensed that the audience had even more anticipation about how what I was about to share might make a difference to them. It is perhaps a small contribution to intentionally adding your own signature to your legacy, but I will avoid having someone simply read my bio as an introduction. Somehow, someway I want them to share the personal connection and experience they have had with me. Now when someone tasked with responsibility for introducing me asks "what do you want me to say or not say from your resume?", I respond by saying "just tell them what about me connects with something about you".

I have worked for and with many leaders who have accomplished a range of things from underperforming to competently maintaining, to commendable difference making. From a leadership standpoint, the one variable that separates the best from the rest has been, what is their legacy? Who took what that leader gave and went above and beyond what they or that leader might have imagined?

Perhaps it is contradictory to propose that one could or should intentionally write their own legacy. It will be up to others to recognize, remember, re-tell what you have done. If you really have left *your leadership signature* on others, they will leave theirs on others as well.

We build our temples for tomorrow, strong as we know how, and we stand on top of the mountain, free within ourselves.

—Langston Hughes

Chapter 7

SIGNATURE SOURCES

Accessing information to define leadership

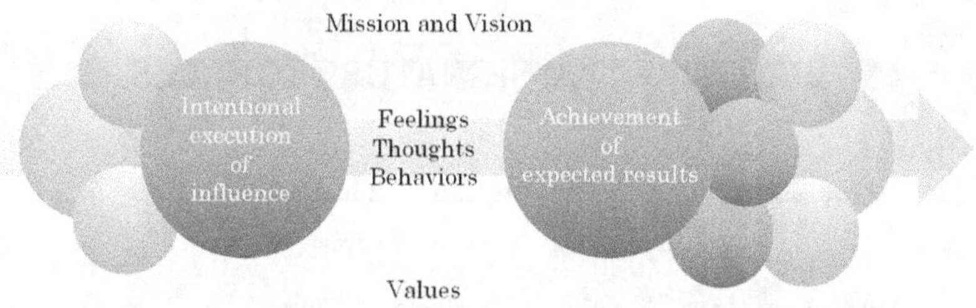

Every experience contributes to defining leadership.
Some leave more defining impressions than others.

Usually the references section of a book serves to validate the sources of information the author has accessed in the process of researching and writing their book. It is where the author acknowledges some of the ideas they raised originated with someone else or were framed in a particular way by another person. It also provides the reader with suggestions of where they may go for more information.

The list of references you find here are different. This section is intended to share with you a list of 20 sources of information that I believe made significant contributions to defining my leadership signature. In some instances, you will find references to books that speak directly to models of leadership and models of effectiveness that support leadership. It also includes works of fiction, religion, philosophy, arts, and other categories whose commonality is that they are written sources that shaped me and shaped me as a leader. You will find them on my book shelves and in easy reach. I chose to limit the list to 20 books to force me to be more selective.

They are books I have actually read. They are sources I frequently quote and refer to as I strive to continue to grow as a leader and work to partner with others on their journey to define their leadership signature. I hope you appreciate reading my list and imagining what the list says about me as a person and a leader. More importantly, I hope you take time to choose your defining 20!

PATHWAY 17A: SIGNATURE SOURCES

List the top 20 books that shaped you as a leader.

1. *Art of War*, Sun Tzu.
2. *Autobiography of Malcolm X, as Told to Alex Haley*, Alex Haley.
3. *Bible*, New International Version.
4. *Black Psychology*, Reginal Jones, Editor.
5. *Blink*, Malcolm Gladwell.
6. *Breaking Through*, David Thomas and John Gabarro.
7. *Drawing on the Right Side of the Brain*, Betty Edwards.
8. *Emotional Intelligence*, Daniel Goleman.
9. *Invisible Man*, Ralph Ellison.
10. *Kodokan Judo*, Jigaro Kano.
11. *L'Etranger*, Albert Camus.
12. *Mindset*, The new psychology of success, Carol Dweck, Ph.D.
13. *Native Son*, Richard Wright.
14. *Pedagogy of the Oppressed*, Paulo Freire.
15. *Power: The Inner Experience*, David McClelland.
16. *Senior Leadership Teams, What It Takes to Make Them Great*, Ruth Wageman, Debra Nunes, James Burrus and Richard Hackman.

17. *SPIN Selling*, Neil Rackham.
18. *Their Eyes Were Watching God*, Zora Neale Hurston.
19. *Tribe, On Homecoming and Belonging*, Sabastian Junger.
20. *The Trusted Advisor*, David Maister, Charles Green and Robert Galford.

I know you have read far more than 20 books. You might even insist that it would take more than 20 to accurately represent the published sources of your signature. There is no researched basis for limiting the list to 20. What is insightful is the process you use and the experience you have in thinking through what have you read that has had a lasting impact on who you are and how you lead. Once you have compiled the list, share it with someone who knows you well and someone who has had a more limited exposure to you. Ask them, what would this list of books tell you about the person who said they represent some of the key contributions to defining that person and them as a leader.

PATHWAY 17: YOUR SIGNATURE SOURCES

List the top 20 books that shaped you as a leader

Ask yourself and someone else what does this list tell you about the person who created it

In addition to books there have been key people to influence who you are as a leader.

PATHWAY 18: YOUR SIGNATURE BOOK COVER

Who would make the cover of *your leadership signature* book?

____

____

____

____

____

POSTSCRIPT

Now what

When I began working to develop leadership competencies I was struck with the power of drawing on the personal stories of people recalling when they were effective as leaders and when they were less effective. It was fascinating to define competencies as what differentiated the best from the rest. It helped clients to define leadership expectations, and design overall talent management strategies to select, develop, and leverage their people resources.

It also allowed us to position those insights as individual development targets when the person was able to differentiate when they were at their best and when they were performing at their "rest of the time". Both for myself and those leaders with whom I partnered, I wanted to believe: If I was able to do something once, I have a chance to do it again. If I have come close, I can get closer. If I have made any progress, I can build on it. If I have stumbled, fallen, or even failed, I can learn from it…and along the way I can be even more effective accelerating and elevating the development and effectiveness of others.

What is your story? What is *your leadership signature*? What legacy have you left behind?

Greg Pennington, Ph.D.

Chapter 8

PATHWAYS

Making leadership development intentional

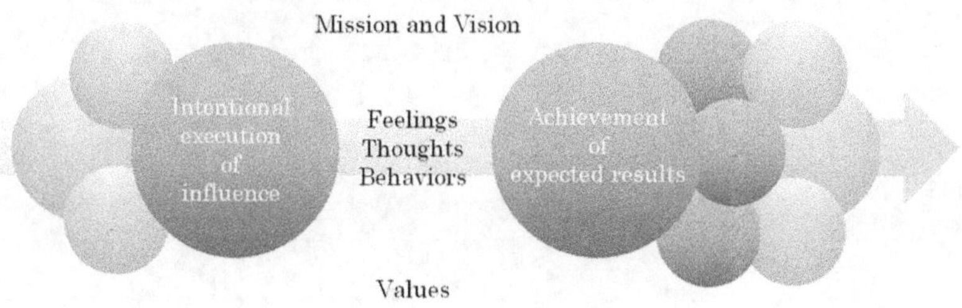

Maps and exercises to find your leadership signature

LEADERSHIP

PATHWAY 1: EXAMPLES OF EFFECTIVE LEADERS

List the names of 3-5 people you consider to be effective leaders.

Describe the types of roles they filled.

Identify specific things they did to make you consider them effective leaders.

Describe how you reacted to what they did. Consider what you felt, thought, and did.

LEADERSHIP

PATHWAY 2: ANALYSIS OF EFFECTIVE LEADERS

What is common in the leaders I chose?

What stands out in the way I describe them?

Cluster the behaviors you described into specific groups.

**Categorize your reactions.

LEADERSHIP

PATHWAY 3: INSIGHTS ON EFFECTIVE LEADERS

How would you describe an effective leader?

LEADERSHIP

PATHWAY 4: YOU AS AN EFFECTIVE LEADER

Why did you or did you not list yourself as an effective leader?

MISSION

PATHWAY 5: LESS DESIRABLE LEADERSHIP MOMENTS

Describe 2-3 Less Desirable Leadership Moments.

What led up to each situation?

What did you feel, think or do?

What was the outcome in each situation?

MISSION

PATHWAY 6: LESS DESIRABLE LEADERSHIP MOMENTS INSIGHTS

What are common elements of the situations you chose to describe?

Identify patterns in what led up to the situations.

What was typical in your reactions?

List any similarities in the outcomes.

What do your situations say about your leadership signature?

MISSION

PATHWAY 7: MORE DESIRABLE LEADERSHIP MOMENTS

Describe 2-3 More Desirable Leadership Moments.

Situation (1)

Situation (2)

Situation (3)

What led up to each situation?

____

____

____

____

____

____

____

____

What did you feel, think, and do?

____

____

____

____

____

____

____

____

What was the outcome in each situation?

MISSION

PATHWAY 8: MORE DESIRABLE LEADERSHIP MOMENTS INSIGHTS

What are common elements of the situations you chose to describe?

Identify patterns in what led up to the situations

Patterns in your reactions

Common thread to the outcomes

What do your situations say about your leadership signature?

MISSION

PATHWAY 9: WHAT IS YOUR WHY

Instead of "what" you do, describe "why" you do.

MISSION

PATHWAY 10: MISSION STATEMENT

I am (adjective describing your greatest virtue – e.g. a leader/doer/ being who is)

Committed to (statement of your purpose)

By (the actions you take)

And by leveraging my strengths of

I will (action items you take)

To achieve (results)

VISION

PATHWAY 11: LEADERS AS READERS

What books have you read in the past year?

What books have you frequently quoted over the past year?

What common themes are apparent in the books you have read and frequently quote?

What does your list say about the way you collect information?

VISION

PATHWAY 12.1: CHOICES AND DECISIONS

Describe 1-2 examples of a personal dilemma.

List three options you had to resolve the dilemma.

What decision criteria did you use to make your choice?

VISION

PATHWAY 12.2: CHOICES AND DECISIONS

Describe 1-2 examples of a direct report or peers dilemma.

List three options you to resolve the dilemma.

What decision criteria did you use to make your choice?

VISION

PATHWAY 12.3: CHOICES AND DECISIONS

Describe 1-2 examples of a leadership team dilemma.

List three options you had to resolve the dilemma.

What decision criteria did you use to make your choice?

VISION

PATHWAY 12.4: ANALYSIS OF CHOICES AND DECISIONS

What themes are common in all three types of dilemmas?

What stands out to you regarding your approach to making choices?

VISION

PATHWAY 13: COMMUNICATION STYLE

What do others say sounds like what you would say?

What do you agree or disagree with?

What are common themes in what others say sounds like you?

What does your communication style indicate about your leadership signature?

IMPACT

PATHWAY 14.1: SOURCES OF POWER

List 2-3 examples of when you said or did something to intentionally influence the behavior of others to achieve a specific result.

Describe what led up to each situation.

What were you feeling or thinking as you considered how to influence
the individuals involved and the outcomes?

IMPACT

PATHWAY 14.2: SOURCES OF POWER

What was the outcome? Consider how the other persons felt and what they thought in reaction to what you did.

How would you describe the sources of power you used?

CAPABILITY

PATHWAY 15.1: TEAM CAPABILITY

List your current team members and what motivates them?

Are there patterns in how you describe what motivates your team members?

What effort do you exert to influence/leverage them?

CAPABILITY

PATHWAY 15.2: TEAM CAPABILITY

Insights from listing the range of options you tend to exercise

Are there options you believe you are unwilling to do?

What insights occur to you when you review the range of options you use to influence your team members?

LEGACY

PATHWAY 16.1: WHAT OTHERS SAY AND REMEMBER ABOUT YOU

List direct reports and peers you have had in last few years.

What would they say about you if asked?

LEGACY

PATHWAY 16.2: WHAT OTHERS SAY AND REMEMBER ABOUT YOU

**List 2-3 teams you led or were a member of recently

How would others describe your team? What was your team known for?

Describe 2-3 team accomplishments you are proud of

How have those accomplishments expanded or been sustained over time?

LEGACY

PATHWAY 16.3: WHAT OTHERS AND REMEMBER ABOUT YOU

What story unfolds that answers the question of what you are known for and remembered for?

LEGACY

PATHWAY 17: YOUR SIGNATURE SOURCES

List the top 20 books that shaped you as a leader

Ask yourself and someone else what does this list tell you about the person who created it

LEGACY

PATHWAY 18: YOUR SIGNATURE BOOK COVER

Who would make the cover of your leadership signature book?

References

1. *Authentic Leadership: Rediscovering the Secrets to Creating Lasting Value*, Bill George, Jossey-Bass, San Francisco.

2. *Dare to Lead: Brave Work. Tough Conversations. Whole Hearts*, Brene Brown, Ph.D., Penguin Random House, LLC, NY.

3. *Destined to Lead, Executive Coaching and Lessons for Leadership Development*, Karol Wasylyshyn, Psy.D. Palgrave Macmillan, NY.

4. *Emotional Intelligence: Why It Can Matter More than IQ*, Daniel Goleman, Bantam Books, NY.

5. *Executive Presence: The Missing Link Between Merit and Success*, Sylvia Ann Hewitt, HarperCollins Publishers, NY.

6. *Immunity to Change: How to Overcome It and Unlock the Potential in Yourself and Your Organization*, Lisa Laskow Lahey and Robert Kegan, Harvard Business Press, Boston.

7. *Influence Redefined: Be the Leader You Were Meant to Be, Monday to Monday*, Stacey Hanke, Greenleaf Book Group Press, Austin.

8. *Leadership That Gets Results*, Daniel Goleman, HBR's 10 Must Reads On Managing People, Harvard Business Review Press, Boston.

9. *Learning Agility: The Key to Leader Potential*, David F. Hoff and W. Warner Burke, Hogan Press.

10. *Mindset, The New Psychology of Success*, Carol Dweck, Random House, LLC, NY.

11. *Narcissistic Leaders: Who Succeeds and Who Fails*, Michael Maccoby, Ph.D, Harvard Business Review Press, Boston.

12. *Power: The Inner Experience*, David McClelland, Irvington Publishers, NY.

13. *Start with Why: How Great Leaders Inspire Everyone to Take Action*, Simon Sinek, Penguin Group, LLC, NY.

14. *Virtuous Leaders, Strategy, Character, and Influence in the 21st Century*, Richard R. Kilburg, Ph.D., American Psychological Association, Washington, DC.